100 Unusual Prompts for Writers of Horror, Weird, and Bizarro Fiction

J.W. DONLEY   (with)   JOHN LANGAN

CARLTON MELLICK III   SHANE HAWK

& more

This goes out to all of my HOWL Society and BizarroCon friends. Stay weird!

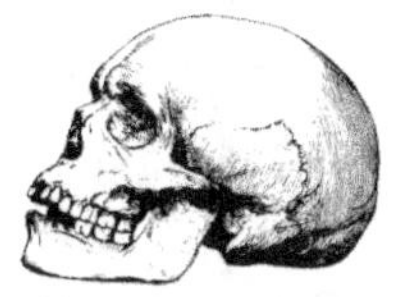

Foreword

As a writer, have you ever found yourself sitting at your computer during your allotted writing time with absolutely no idea what to write? This has happened to me way more times than I care to admit. The weight of complete freedom to write whatever I want is sometimes too much. My brain will forever cycle between different small sparks without spending enough time on one to kindle a real creative fire.

The solution?

For me, it is limiting scope; setting some rules that I must follow or starting with a handful of pre-determined ideas is the key.

This removes the infinity of possibilities from my thoughts, and lets me focus on just a small subset of fantastic creation.

There are tons of writing prompt books out in the wild. And I have a number of them both on my bookshelf, but none are truly targeted to the sort of writing I lean towards. They are more generic and safe. This means no trans-dimensional alien sex scenes, no tentacle-based body horror, and definitely no satanic fast food chain debacles.

Whatever should a writer of the strange and horrifying do?

Well, after attending the 2023 BizzaroCon and meeting so many other writers of the dark, bizarre, and just plain fucked up, I decided to solve this monumental dilemma. I, J.W. Donley, would take on this challenge and produce a book of 100 writing prompts guaranteed to spur us weirdos into a writing frenzy.

So, I started documenting a ton of crazy writing ideas, creating an ever-growing list. Then, it dawned on me. What would truly make a book of ultra weird writing prompts ultra amazing? Answer: Ask friends who also write ultra weird fiction to pitch in an idea or two. I never thought I would get such an enthusiastic response. In these pages there are writing prompts from John Langan, author of *The Fisherman*, Carlton Mellick III, author of bizzaro staples like *The Haunted Vagina*, *The Baby Jesus Butt Plug*, and *Satan Burger*, and Ai Jiang, author of *Linghun*, and so many many more. I couldn't be happier with the book you now hold in your hands.

Now, you know what to do. Flip this book to a random page and get inspired!

J.W. Donley
Bellingham, WA
March 21st, 2024

How to Use
This Book

There are prompts of all sorts within these pages. Some are only a line or two long, others are multiple pages of instructions. Some are just an image and one is a prompt with a million possibilities.

You can choose a prompt in a handful of ways. The first, and most boring, way is to just go through the book, one by one. The next is to just flip it open at random. Last, and my favorite, is to roll a d100. You can do this using your dice set from playing table top role playing games using two ten-sided dice. The first dice represents the tens digit, while the second represents the one. For example if you roll a 9 and a 2 you get 92. Or if you roll a 10 and a 5 you get 5 (this is because a 10 rolled in the tens digit represents zero).

If you don't have a set of dice this website will choose a random number for you from 1 through 100: https://www.calculatorsoup.com/calculators/statistics/random-number-generator-1-100.php

The Prompts

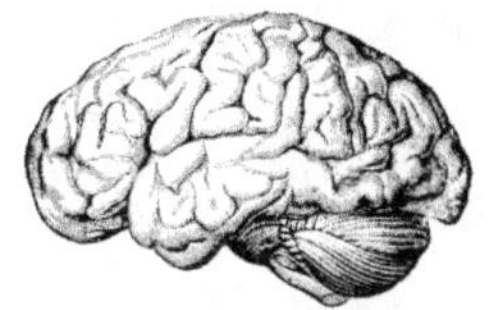

Prompt 1

Pugs suddenly develop a hive mind and decide humans are no longer worthy to be their owners. Except you. Your pug has judged you worthy. But no one else, not even loved ones. What do you do?

Prompt 2

Make the preparation of last night's dinner an epic mis-adventure.

Prompt 3

Start a story with this dialogue:

"And so, I stood there half naked, holding a stolen plastic baby Jesus filled with tapioca pudding..."

Prompt 4

Carlton Mellick III

This is how I come up with the majority of my book ideas:

First, pick up a random book off of your book shelf. On a random page, without looking, point at a random word and write it down. Do this about 10-20 times or until you fill up a sheet of paper. Now combine two or three of these words, also at random. The more unusual the combination the better. Whichever combination of words intrigues you most, use that as the title of a story. Imagine what the most interesting and unpredictable story would go with that title. Then write it.

This is the method I used to write my books Satan Burger, Quicksand House, Hungry Bug, War Slut, Cuddly Holocaust, Armadillo Fists, Hammer Wives, Parasite Milk, and even The Haunted Vagina, among many others.

Prompt 5

What's the craziest thing that could happen at the DMV in a horror movie?

Prompt 6

Write a sex scene that starts out spicy, but devolves into existential dread and cosmic horror, but the POV is still into it.

Prompt 7

Write a sex scene that starts out 'meh' but develops into astral ascension.

Prompt 8

Bridget D. Brave

You awake to discover your legs have begun to dissolve into puddles. Worse yet, no one seems to understand why this is a problem.

Prompt 9

Cats.

What is their ultimate agenda? No, really! Please tell me!

Prompt 10

How does this banana make you feel?

Prompt 11

Clay Vermulm

You're the last remaining member of a doomed expedition. Could be in space, Antarctica, an island in the middle of the ocean or a high mountain pass, take your pick. You've had to do inexplicable things to survive, but you have lived. One such inexplicable thing was, regrettably, cannibalism. At least Old' Frank won't be bothering you anymore, right? Wrong. Too bad you'll never get to have a fire-side heart to heart with Phyllis again, eh? Wrong again. Tell the story of this doomed survivalist who is now inhabited by the souls and voices of those they had to consume to survive. Whether said souls consented to their consumption, is up to you. I mean if we are ever in the mountains together, I die of natural causes, and you need to eat me to survive, I'd totally endorse that decision. But like, don't murder me unless I say it's cool, OK? That's just rude.

Prompt 12

What if all horrible creatures drawn in medieval marginalia were real? And there was a zoo for them somewhere in the Midwestern US?

Prompt 13

Go watch your favorite movie. During the credits write down every aspect of that movie that makes it awesome. Don't stop writing until the credits stop.

Prompt 14

P.L. McMillan

(Please turn the page for your prompt...)

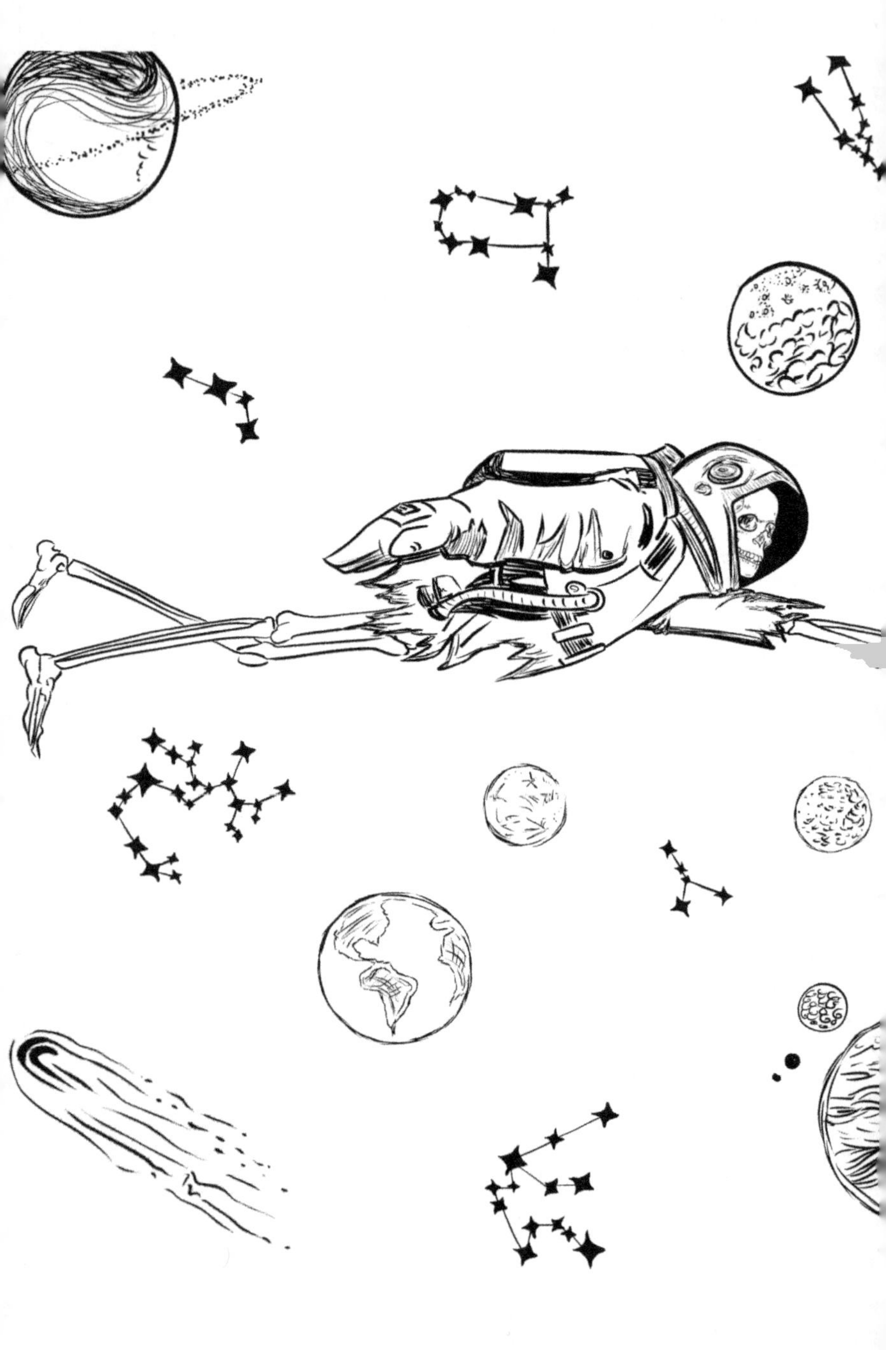

P.L. MCMILLAN

Prompt 15

The spot on your forehead over your pineal gland itches. You check a mirror and see a long black hair. You pull, and it comes out like a long knotted string. You feel each knot as it passes through the hole in your head, like morse code. You have yards of knotted string before it ends. What message is recorded in the knots?

Prompt 16

Go to your fridge. Pick out a random sauce or condiment from the door. Look on the back and see what city it was packaged in. Do a quick Wikipedia search on the city, and imagine what life would be like working at that packaging plant as the city devolves into chaos. Asteroid heading toward earth and hitting in a few weeks? Ocean levels dropping continuously at a high rate? Solar flare knocks out all electric grids? You decide!

Prompt 17

Shane Hawk

Your main character is a spirit hunter and is in a new location for the week. They use a ouija board to ask if anyone is present.

Something replies yes, and they ask the spirit, "What year is it for you?"

The spirit responds "2094. Are you a ghost?"

Prompt 18

Go to a random Wikipedia article 2-3 times. You can use this link to pull one up at random: https://en.wikipedia.org/wiki/Special: Random

Force a connection between them to form a story.

For example: I pulled articles for

- The song "The Chamber" by Lenny Kravitz — https://en.wikipedia.org/ wiki/The_Chamber_(song)

- *Pyrausta carnifex* — https://en.wikipedia.org/wiki/Pyrausta_carnifex
- The Rukmavati River — https://en.wikipedia.org/wiki/Rukmavati_River

Prompt 19

Christi Nogle

Families are pretty scary in general, and family photos even more so. Do you have a drawer or a box somewhere with a bunch of old family photos in it? If so, spend an hour or so finding the creepiest one and write a story about it. If you don't, ask your friends for their creepy family photos. If you don't have friends, you can use my creepy family photo on the next page. Enjoy!

Prompt 20

Go outside! That's it. No pressure to write. Just take a break and enjoy not being cooped up. You can write afterward if you'd like.

Prompt 21

Describe the process of eating a hot dog with all of your favorite toppings, but in reverse. (All of the way back as far as you would like. Maybe even through harvesting of the grain for the bun.)

Prompt 22

John Baltisberger

Write a poem about how a Kaiju destroyed your love life.

Prompt 23

Prompt 24

tibi sitüt et ego patet
filijs notam facietur
uitatem tua... o
mine saluü me fac
et psalmos nostros

Prompt 25

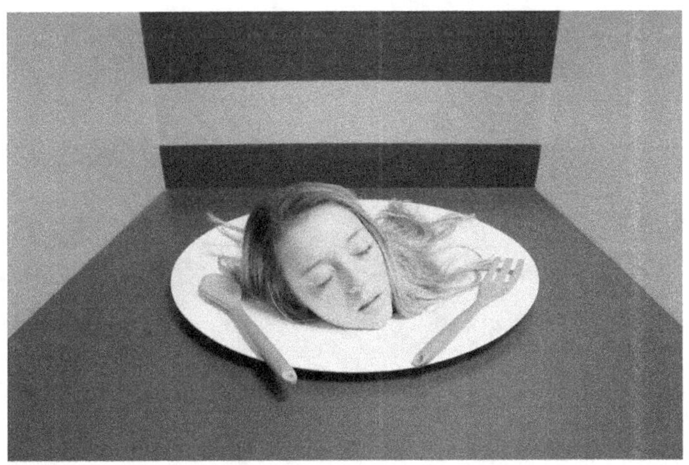

Prompt 26

Ai Jiang

(Please turn the page for your prompt...)

NAME OF PASSENGER
LEUK OCYTES
DATE
SEPT. 13, 5931
SEAT
725019
123 456 789 10 11 12
BONE
MARROW
INT
ONE-WAY EMERGENCY BOARDING PA
PLEASE HEAD TO THE BOARDING GATE IMMEDIATEL

#731
PILOT
AI JIANG

TIUM,

LUNG

FIRST
CLASS

PASSENGER
LEUK OCYTES

BOARDING TIME
EMERGENCY

GATE
CAPILLARIES

FLIGHT
#731

FROM
BONE MARROW

TO
INTERSTITIUM, LUNG

Prompt 27

There's a zombie outbreak, but it isn't affecting humans. Instead, chickens are rising from the dead in supermarkets across the globe.

Prompt 28

An event has definitively proven to the Vatican that (mythology of your choice) is real and the church has redirected accordingly. Describe the event.

Prompt 29

Richard Thomas

This is your surrealism prompt. Take a character and replace them with any animal, do not explain why. Yes, they may talk, but they don't HAVE to. Take a page from Salvador Dali and incorporate one image from his paintings (such as a melting clock). Take an iconic image from Renee Magritte and replace a body part with a fruit or vegetable (such as a head replaced with a green apple). And finally add a Brian Evenson "fourth element." In writing there is a thing known as the rule of threes, which is 'a story-telling principle that suggests people better understand concepts, situations, and ideas in groups of three.' Brian Evenson often uses a FOURTH (or FIFTH) element—often going beyond the concrete into the abstract and surreal. For example, in his story "Windeye" an older brother asks his sister to put her fingers up under a shingle of their house. The first questions are normal—is it smooth, does it feel rough. Then it starts to get weirder. Scaly? Warm-blooded or cold-blooded. And finally, does it feel red? This is anthropomorphism, making an inanimate object feel alive. And also, how the hell does something FEEL RED? Incorporate all four challenges in your story. Good luck!

Prompt 30

You know that corner bodega store in town that you never see anyone go into? Go there! Then come back and describe the experience. What did it smell like? What sort of products did they sell that you've never seen elsewhere?

Prompt 31

What is the most disgusting thing that a magician could accidentally pull out of his hat?

Prompt 32

Chris O'Halloran

Take two random books from your bookshelf and combine the premises.

Example:

The Shining and Dune = A father battling addiction must protect his family from the sandworms burrowing into the hotel for which he is the caretaker.

Or

Harry Potter and Silence of the Lambs = A talented boy wizard is the key to finding the location of a dangerous serial killer holding the headmaster hostage.

Prompt 33

Look at the 3rd, 7th, and 13th most recent images on your phone's camera roll. What story do they tell as a beginning, middle, and end?

Prompt 34

What would be the most interesting murder weapon that you've never seen used in a slasher film, and why?

Prompt 35

Describe a scene where your favorite slasher movie villain suddenly drops into your favorite childhood cartoon show.

Prompt 36

Angela Sylvaine

A person stands before a mirror and punches themself in the face, causing their brittle skin to crack like thin china. The proceed to wedge their fingers beneath the skin and peel it off piece by piece like an egg shell.

Prompt 37

Describe the autopsy of a whimsical and/or mythological creature. How did it die?

Prompt 38

Take an uncomfortable nap. For some reason some of my most vivid dreams happen when I sleep in almost comfy places. Like out in your car in the driveway. When you wake up take notes on your delirious dreams.

Prompt 39

John Baltisberger

Clippy the Microsoft assistant is given AI, and he is extremely horny.

Prompt 40

A voice starts speaking around you, narrating every move you make. But then states: 'Little did they know, ____'. Fill in the blank and what they do next.

Prompt 41

That's it, the cocoa plant is now extinct. Your character works in the ultra bougie business of reselling some of the last chocolate on the planet. What is their daily life like? What are the dangers?

Prompt 42

Go pet a doggo. Guaranteed to make you feel less stressed and give you the energy to destroy your writer's block.

Prompt 43

Sam Rebelein

Many paranormal/monster stories revolve around the emotional experience of grief, using the monster/ghost as a symbol for that grief. Write a story in which a DIFFERENT emotion (joy, disgust, anger, hunger, etc.) is symbolized by something tangible and horrific. Think about how that emotion feels in your body and translate that into an antagonistic force. For example, when I'm hungry, I feel my stomach yawning for food. Maybe there's a cave in the woods that roars for food, or a swarm of mosquitos with a never ending lust for blood. Go nuts! You can also do this same prompt with a particular anxiety: What specific, tangible fear can act as an emotional symbol for, say, dying alone, or having your kid kidnapped, or getting rejected by a potential date?

Prompt 44

You discover that your family has been using your prosthetic leg to smuggle drugs. But, you never knew you had a prosthetic until you are stopped by a drug dog at the Canadian border.

Prompt 45

Your tapeworm is the telepathic reincarnation of [insert your choice of historic figure here] and you've become best friends. What sort of adventures do the two of you go on?

Prompt 46

John Langan

Here is a partial list of recent-ish anthologies in which I have not appeared:

- *After: Nineteen Stories of Apocalypse and Dystopia*
- *Armored: Part Human, Part Machine, All Soldier*
- *The Beastly Bride: Tales of the Animal People*
- *Black Feathers: Dark Avian Tales*
- *Body Shocks: Extreme Tales of Body Horror*
- *The Book of Dragons*
- *Brave New Worlds*

- *Classic Monsters Unleashed*
- *Close to Midnight*
- *Cold War Cthulhu*
- *Cosmic Powers: The Saga Anthology of Far-Away Galaxies*
- *The Coyote Road: Trickster Tales*
- *Cursed*
- *The Cutting Room: Dark Reflections on the Silver Screen*
- *The Dark of the Woods: Fairy Tales for Modern Times*
- *Darker Companions: Celebrating 50 Years of Ramsey Campbell*
- *Dead Letters: Episodes of Epistolary Horror*
- *Dead Man's Hand: An Anthology of the Weird West*
- *Deepest Darkest Eden: New Tales of Hyperborea*
- *Disintegration*
- *The Drive-In: Multiplex*
- *Euroschlock Nightmares*
- *The Faery Reel: Tales from the Twilight Realm*

- *Flight or Fright: 17 Turbulent Tales*
- *Found: An Anthology of Found Footage Horror Stories*
- *Full Moon City*
- *Haunted Legends*
- *Hauntings*
- *His Own Most Fantastic Creation: Stories about H.P. Lovecraft*
- *Howls from the Dark Ages: An Anthology of Medieval Horror*
- *Human Monsters*
- *The Improbable Adventures of Sherlock Holmes*
- *In Heaven, Everything is Fine: Fiction Inspired by David Lynch*
- *In the Court of the Yellow King*
- *Inferno: Tales of Terror and the Supernatural*
- *Isolation*
- *The Living Dead 2*
- *Lost Films*
- *Lost Signals*
- *Lost Worlds and Mythological Kingdoms*

- *Lovecraft Unbound*
- *Mad Hatters and March Hares: All-New Stories from the World of Lewis Carroll's Alice in Wonderland*
- *The Mad Scientist's Guide to World Domination: Original Short Fiction for the Modern Evil Genius*
- *Mountains of Madness Revealed*
- *Naked City: Tales of Urban Fantasy*
- *The New Flesh: A Literary Tribute to David Cronenberg*
- *New Maps of Dream*
- *The New Space Opera*
- *Nightmare Carnival*
- *Operation Arcana*
- *Other Worlds than These*
- *Oz Reimagined: New Tales from the Emerald City and Beyond*
- *Pluto in Furs*
- *Psychos: Serial Killers, Depraved Madmen, and the Criminally Insane*
- *Queen Victoria's Book of Spells: An Anthology of Gaslamp Fantasy*

- *Return of the Old Ones: Apocalyptic Lovecraftian Horror*
- *Ride the Star Wind: Cthulhu, Space Opera, and the Cosmic Weird*
- *Robot Uprisings*
- *Salon Fantastique*
- *Shadows Out of Time*
- *Shakespeare Unleashed*
- *Shotguns v. Cthulhu*
- *Sirens and Other Daemon Lovers: Magical Tales of Love and Seduction*
- *Tails of Wonder and Imagination: Cat Stories*
- *Tales from the Crust: An Anthology of Pizza Horror*
- *Tales from the Miskatonic University Library*
- *Teeth: Vampire Tales*
- *Test Patterns: Creature Features*
- *Tomorrow's Cthulhu: Stories at the Dawn of Posthumanity*
- *Troll's Eye View: A Book of Villainous Tales*

- *Twice Cursed*
- *Under the Moons of Mars: New Adventures on Barsoom*
- *Vanishing Acts*
- *Wastelands 2*
- *Wastelands: The New Apocalypse*
- *The Way of the Wizard*
- *A Wolf at the Door and Other Retold Fairy Tales*
- *Wonderland: An Anthology of Works Inspired by Alice's Adventures in Wonderland*
- *World War Cthulhu: A Collection of Lovecraftian War Stories*

The point of this list is not the airing of grievances. In many cases, I was invited to the anthology in question, and either couldn't come up with a story for it or couldn't finish the story I had started by the deadline. In other cases, the editor(s) didn't think of my name in connection with the anthology's topic. In still other cases, the editor(s) didn't think I would be a good fit for the book they were putting together. In a very few cases, the editor(s) didn't think I would accept an invitation to their small-press effort. (Which is insane, by the way.)

The point of listing these titles is to offer them to you, the writer in search of inspiration, as sources for exactly that. To explain what I mean, a brief bit of personal history:

When I started to publish my fiction professionally (very slowly, it must be said, a story a year from 2001-2003 and then nothing again until 2007), I would read reviews of anthologies and wish I had been invited to them; I would read about open calls for anthologies and wish I could write fast enough to meet their deadlines; I would read or hear friends talking about being invited to this or that anthology and ask myself why I hadn't received an invitation. In the future, I said to myself, should anyone send me an invitation to an anthology, I would accept it.

This plan, it seems, worked: I've published a number of stories in a number of anthologies. But as the list above shows, I have not been part of many more. Rather than stew in resentment or self-recrimination, however, I've chosen to think of these titles as something else, namely, as prompts for stories, and this is where my personal history converges with the point of this essay. To give an example: just because I wasn't invited to contribute to a volume on the subject of Queen Victoria's book of spells doesn't mean I can't write something on the topic. (Indeed, I've read enough Victorian poetry and prose that I could probably come up with something pretty decent.) The same is true when it comes to Sherlock Holmes, whose adventures I read avidly in middle school, and Barsoom, the Mars of Edgar Rice Burroughs's John Carter. Ramsey Campbell is a titan of weird fiction, and while I nosed around a story for *Darker Companions*, I was never able to nail down exactly how I was going to do what I wanted to do. (Though I might finally have figured something out.) At one point, I think it was Del Rey who reissued a number of the Oz books, which I read and found deeply odd; the idea of writing something set in those strange lands is deeply appealing. And dragons? Who doesn't want to write a story about a dragon?

In a few instances, these prompts have resulted in stories which I've then published in other anthologies. The *Armored* idea, for example, grew into a story called "Second Front," which appeared in an anthology called *Weird War III*. The various Alice in Wonderland books resulted in a story called "Alice's Rebellion," which was published in *After Sundown*. To be honest, there isn't a title among the ones I've listed, and several more besides, that doesn't make me wonder what kind of story I would write for it. Some titles suggest very specific scenarios, particularly the various apocalyptic and post-apocalyptic ones; others are more nebulous. How would you go about writing a story in David Cronenberg mode, for example? Or David Lynch?

Here's a practical exercise: pick five of the titles I've listed and write a one paragraph response to it. Maybe it's the very beginning of the story; maybe it's from some-where deeper within; maybe it's the very end. From these, pick the three that work best for you and expand your paragraph into a page. From the three, pick the two you think are strongest and stick with them for another page or two. Then pick the one you feel is working best and finish it.

(If you're feeling up for a challenge, do the same exercise with what seem to you the five worst ideas for a story. Sometimes, I have to be honest, the less promising an idea for a story is, the more intrigued I am by it. Your milage may vary, as the kids say.)

Think of all the anthologies you've read and read of as being only partially complete. What they're waiting for is you.

Prompt 47

A generic version of your favorite super hero confronts a cult worshipping a Lovecraftian monstrosity of your choice.

Prompt 48

You run a travel agency specializing in alien sex tourism across the galaxy. What is in your brochure?

Prompt 49

Frances Lu-Pai Ippolito

<u>Making New Friends</u>

Follow a stranger in a public place for five minutes without being discovered. This may be done by watching someone at a café or restaurant, or by following someone in a grocery store, library, or museum. Caveat: do not follow minors.

During the five minutes, mentally record all the details you observe about the person—clothing, mannerisms, facial expressions, voice, how they eat or walk, etc.

After the five minutes have passed, do three writing exercises:

1. Five minutes free writing about all
    the details about the person.
2. Five minutes free writing about
    your own experience following a
    stranger.
3. Ten minutes free writing a story
    using 1), 2), or both.

Prompt 50

It is now law that zombies are still considered US citizens. Now we must ethically feed them. You work for a company that harvests brains. What is your day to day life like?

Prompt 51

Cannibalism is now legal under extreme circumstances. What are some grey areas still not fully defined by the law as written? And how are these laws enforced?

Prompt 52

S.A. Hunt

In 1940s Nebraska, a young city-slicker farmer discovers an ominous grave beyond his cornfield. Neither his preacher brother or Sioux ranchhand will go near it, but when his scarecrow starts showing up in weird places, his livestock turns up dead, and his pregnant wife begins to behave strangely, the farmer finds himself in a battle of wits with the thing buried in the woods.

Prompt 53

Necromancy is heavily controlled by government agencies and used to bring back the dead who are worthy. What makes a person worthy to be brought back to life? How much would this service cost on the black market?

Prompt 54

The next big fad is to gamble using dice made from your own bones.

Prompt 55

Clay Vermulm

Do that thing where you spin a globe and stop it with your finger. Wherever you land is the last outpost of a dwindling human population after whatever devastating apocalypse you care to dream up. Or is it?! Spin the globe again. The second location is where there is said to be a survivalist city with food, water, attractive people to have sex with, and streets paved in mattresses. Tell the story of the journey from point A (for apocalypse) to point P (for paradise). Again, whether it's really there, or whether people ACTUALLY go looking for it, or get anywhere close, is totally your call.

Prompt 56

<u>Mood Pimples</u>

A new candy causes the pus inside your pimples to change color depending on your mood.

Prompt 57

Describe a sunset over rolling hills of teeth.

Prompt 58

Caleb Stephens

Write a story from the perspective of an ailment or a disease. This could be anything from a common cold or a headache, to something far more sinister, like cancer or Alzheimer's. What are its dastardly hopes and dreams? What does it want to accomplish in life? It is, after all, just trying to exist like the rest of us.

Prompt 59

You've won a contest and now have the opportunity to transfer your consciousness into a dog. What breed of dog would you choose, and who would be your owner?

Prompt 60

What is something that scares you that others
to do not understand?

Put a hat on it.

Did that help?

Prompt 61

Michael Allen Rose

Wait until you are home alone, with nobody else around. Find an interior room with no windows, no outside light sources, no escape but through the door through which you entered. A bathroom, or a closet, somewhere you can sit in the quiet and darkness and just be. A crack of light underneath the door should be the maximum illumination. A bathroom is ideal, because you need to find a large mirror. If there isn't one installed on the wall or a cabinet, a large hand mirror will be fine, so long as you can prop it up somewhere and face it. Sit down in the darkness, relax, and stare into the mirror. It doesn't matter that you can't really see anything. You will. Be patient, and sit, staring into the reflection. Try to find your reflection's eyes, and stare into the eyes of your other self. Continue to look. Wait, while your eyes begin to adjust to the darkness. Eventually, you'll start to see your reflection staring back at you. Quietly wait. Breathe. Maintain eye contact. Use your peripheral vision to study the obscured details around your face, how the features look like yours but not, how the vision distorts and warps. Allow yourself to relax, to empty yourself of intention. Eventually, the creature in the mirror will start to shift. Details will look unfamiliar. Your passport to the uncanny valley has arrived. Keep staring. Who is this creature in the mirror? This is your new antagonist/protagonist. What does it want? What will make it go away? Why did you let it in? Is it dangerous? Where will it go from here? How is it different from you? If you move, will it let you? It is here now, and your only recourse is to write about it.

Prompt 62

Go to a used bookstore and visit a section with books of a genre you usually do not read. Choose one book at random from this section and read the back. How could you change things to make it a cosmic horror, slasher horror, or Bizarro story?

Prompt 63

Some people have an exact opposite of themself roaming the Earth right now. What cataclysmic event would happen if they met?

Prompt 64

Brianna Malotke

You're laying in bed trying to sleep with your partner snoring soundly next to you. You hear them start to murmur in their sleep. They roll over, facing you now and start talking to the Devil. They say, "I can't sacrifice them to you Satan, I can't." Your partner suddenly grabs your arm, clinging to you, their eyes still closed. They murmur "I won't kill them...yet."

What happens next?

Prompt 65

Tell me about the clairvoyant mole on the back of your head.

Prompt 66

Tell us why you know how many ferrets it takes to condemn a whole town.

Prompt 67

TJ Price

Go On, Ask the Shadows

a prompt for generative writing

Some of my best work has originated from generative thinking, from haphazard huckle-berrying through the bristly fields of my own brain with only the horizon as my boundary, but I must admit that I never feel more free than when I am playing within the idea of limitations. This might seem like a bit of a paradox, but hear me out. It's certainly not an original thought—I learned about the ideas of imposing arbitrary rules on writing via reading those from the Oulipo group (*ouvroir de littérature potentielle*; translated loosely, "workshop of potential literature,") who employed the nature of restrictions or parameters on their creativity to trigger ideas for further investigation and development. One of the best-known members of Oulipo, Georges Perec, managed to use this to his advantage—he wrote a novel with the proviso that there is never once a single occurrence of the letter "E." Cannily, he also managed to work this omission into narrative itself—the story concerns the sudden disappearance of one Anton Vowl, and dips its toe into not only the mystery genre, but also contains elements of horror and noir fiction as well. (It's also surprisingly readable, and at one point even contains an entire re-writing of Edgar Allan Poe's "The Raven," while still adhering to Perec's lipogrammatic limitation.)

I also often find that limitations can cause us to narrow our focus on elements that might inhabit a blind spot in our craft. For example, if I told you to write a story without using the word "you," dost thou think it might be a bit difficult? Forced to resort to other methods of expression rather than defaulting to the norm, one might find themselves suddenly able to extrapolate this modality of thought to other, less-traversed paths of expression—and so on, and so on.

Thus, the prompt I provide here is one of *constraint*.

In our modern era, there is an abundance of weight placed on the value of answers—but what about their progenitor—the *question*? A good prompt should be something that changes one's perspective, jostles the kaleidoscope of the mind's eye, and there's no better way to see different patterns than by asking a question. There's also nothing more horrific than an unanswered—or even *unanswerable*—question.

This is supposed to be a horror-specific prompt, though, so I'll hasten to add: there is nothing that we fear more than the unknown; that which lives beyond the edges of our comprehension—so invite it in. Sit down and ask a question. It can be anything—maybe even the first thing that bubbles to the surface of your mind—but follow where the tail of that first question mark leads. For example—

How sharp is a tooth?

What has teeth?

If it lives in the dark, can I see its teeth?

Did I just hear a voice?

Am I alone in the house?

Am I alone in the room?

And so on. Resist the urge to answer these questions—allow your mind to entertain possibilities for each, but soon enough you will find a question that your brain can seize on. (Psychiatrists call this 'catastrophizing,' I call it 'storytelling.')

So, ask yourself something. See what rises out of the murk to meet your inquiry.

It might even end up being a story.

Prompt 68

Grocery shopping is now a full contact televised event.

Prompt 69

What is the origin story of the cult with that always empty building on main street?

Prompt 70

S.A. Hunt

"We're with Publisher's Clearinghouse," he said as I invited him into the house, "and you've won a million dollars!"

"I thought Ed McMahon died in 2009," I said, just before the man holding the giant check sank his teeth into my husband's throat.

Before the night was through, I would earn the hell out of that money.

Prompt 71

Take your 3 (or more) favorite conspiracy theories and combine them into one mega theory involving either alien invasion or demonic possession.

Prompt 72

Every time you get that weird sense of deja vu, an alternate universe version of you has died, and now you can visit that universe. What would you do while there?

Prompt 73

Patrick Barb

<u>Protagonist/Antagonist Swap</u>

Pick your favorite movie/book/story, etc. in the genre you're writing in, and brainstorm a story where the protagonist and antagonist roles are swapped. Think Halloween, but it's about a masked man who just wants to go home and he's being stalked by murderous babysitting teens.

Prompt 74

Go to the public library and find a librarian. Ask them what is the weirdest book they've ever come across on the job. Write a story explaining why this book exists and how it will one day save humanity.

Prompt 75

Humanity has found a way to condense a living human body into a one foot cube with the head left in its original size, the arms and legs deflated into dangling semi-functional appendages. This makes it easy to densely store sleeping, comatose, and dead individuals in massive warehouses. The process is reversible within a few days with no known side effects. How does this affect the world's over-population problem? What are some ways this new procedure manifests in human culture? What happens to those accidentally left in this state too long.

Prompt 76

Carson Winter

<u>Write what you hate</u>

We all love horror—except when we don't.

Slashers are predictable; vampires are over-sexed bores. We ball our fists up with rage when the nice family's pet is murdered by ghosts. We balk at the idiots going down into the basement after their friend was brutally murdered.

Horror is filled with ideas, but not every one of them is good.

This exercise though is about tackling

those eye-rollingly terrible ideas and chal-
lenging, transforming, and reinventing them.

For best results, pick something that you
truly hate. A horror subgenre or trope that
you'd usually never touch.

Write a zombie story where a zombie
never appears on the page. Write a story
about cosmic horror where the Necronomicon
is found by a kindly old bookseller in a dona-
tion bin. Tired of woe-is-me werewolf tales?
Time to write a fuck-yeah werewolf tale.

Twist old, tired stories into something
new.

Prompt 77

A incompetent serial killer is menacing a small town, but for some reason (sheer luck) he is never caught. What finally gets him caught?

Prompt 78

Why does your uncle keep 50 pound bags of birdseed in his house when birds have been extinct for over 20 years.

Prompt 79

C.B. Jones

Think back to a time in your childhood where you stumbled into a location or environment that you either weren't supposed to be in or just felt wrong or surreal: the elementary school after hours, an older sibling's teenage party, an abandoned construction site, a restricted area in your favorite mall, the weird religious ceremony you witnessed in the field that you always used as a shortcut on your way home. Use this environment as a setting or a jumping off point for your story.

Prompt 80

How do you keep kids from eating their own teeth when they taste so amazing?

Prompt 81

All tow truck drivers are members of a secret organization with many warring factions. What happens when a member of one faction accidentally does business in the wrong territory?

Prompt 82

John Baltisberger

A man arrives at a mosque demanding a the Imam perform a wedding for two people who have obviously been kidnapped.

Prompt 83

Cats are the size of horses and are the primary mode of transportation. What is the daily commute like in the big city?

Prompt 84

Write the most predictable ghost story you can. Make this fit on one page. Use every trope. This will get it out of your system so you can create crazy original stuff.

Prompt 85

Frances Lu-Pai Ippolito

Provide 1-2 captions for the figures on the following pages. Use the captions in a seven (7) minute free write.

WITNESSES:
J. W. Garfield
E. M. Clark

INVENTOR:
R. J. Spalding.
BY
Munn & Co
ATTORNEYS.

R. J. SPALDING.
FLYING MACHINE.

No. 398,984.
Patented Mar. 5, 1889.

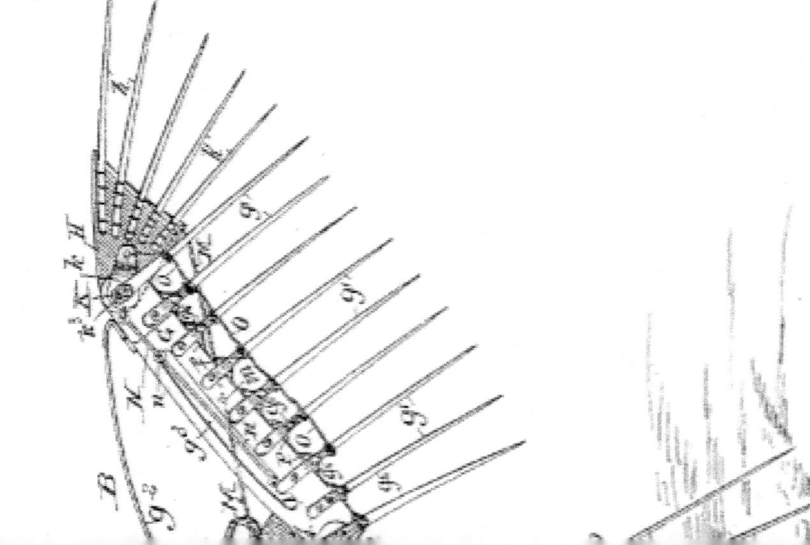

R. J. SPALDING.
FLYING MACHINE.

No. 398,984.   Patented Mar. 5, 1889.

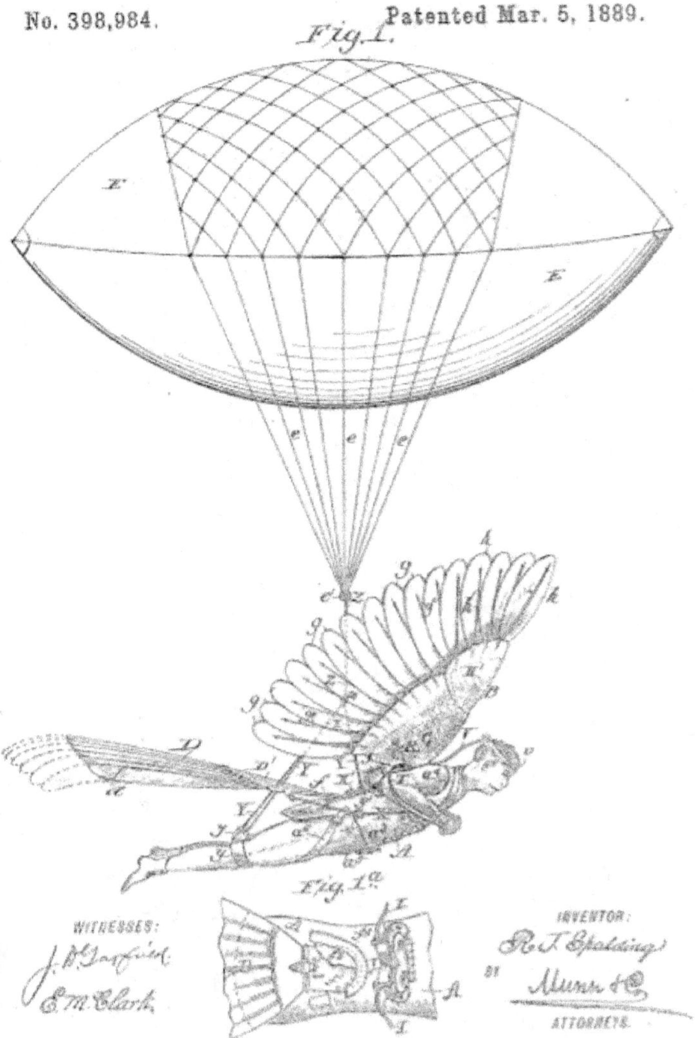

WITNESSES:
J. D. Garfield.
E. M. Clark.

INVENTOR:
R. J. Spalding
BY
Munn & Co.
ATTORNEYS.

Prompt 86

Write the most explicit, kinky, graphic sex scene you can possibly scrounge from that amazing brain of yours. Don't worry. No one but you will read this, unless you decide to share. Free write without stopping for at least twenty minutes. When you are done, read over your creation. Feel free to nuke it from orbit at this point, or file it away for later use.

Prompt 87

Do the same exercise as prompt 86, but add more and more active parties. Change it up, add aliens, reptile people, whatever.

Prompt 88

Chelsea Pumpkins

There are horrors and marvels alike that reside under your skin, neatly and courteously hidden from view. But now the viscera typically contained within the cage of your skeleton; liters of fluids, meters of organs; tissues and tendons and peculiar abnormalities... It is all exposed. Lean into the taboo and abjection of your insides being outside.

Prompt 89

It turns out that cancer cells taste delicious. What is it like visiting a black market for purchasing this very illegal ingredient?

Prompt 90

Describe, with excruciating detail, the process of removing your own eye due to an insane emergency situation using the kitchen utensil of your choice.

Prompt 91

S.A. Hunt

A high school student discovers that the pristine mascot costume he found in the school gym's storage closet is indestructible.

Prompt 92

Summarize Alice in Wonderland, but as a much more bizarro/horror story.

Prompt 93

A black sun rises over a scorched landscape. A cacophony of trumpets blare from the four directions carried on the four winds of plague. Those who still remain, tremble and weep. The last revelation approaches yet there are those who still rally and fight the inevitable end of all. What is their story?

Prompt 94

Garrett A. Cook

Write a scene in which no object serves its traditional purpose. If someone sits on a chair, you have failed the exercise. If someone sits on a hand or an ostrich, you're getting it. Try to make as many set-pieces and objects counterintuitive and wrong as you can.

Prompt 95

You have an SSD hard drives installed in one of your sinus cavities. What sort of data do you keep stored there?

Prompt 96

Aliens have invaded, but it wasn't a big deal. Life carries on. We still have bills, jobs, and taxes. Just, now there's also weird green over-lords controlling all governments. They were in control before the invasion, but now they do it openly.

Prompt 97

Shane Hawk

A small town's well-known puppeteer dies mysteriously. When called in to investigate, your main character detective realizes the marionettes are all made from human skin and hair. Every time he picks one up by its strings, the detective experiences a vision that reveals secrets about the townspeople who have been reported as missing.

Prompt 98

A secret organization of those who survived serial killers have discovered the location for the next international serial killer summit. Describe the events that transpire at that summit.

Prompt 99

How many times have you walked out your front door, and the world was there, just as expected. Every morning, you get ready for work then step out into the day ready to dive in. But, what would you do if the world was different? Not in any way you could describe. But you know it is different and this makes you uncomfortable.

Prompt 100

Ultimate Triple d100 Randomizer of DOOM!

Below are three lists: the first with 100 objects, the second with 100 characters, and the third with 100 settings. Choose one entry from each list at random and use those to brainstorm, then craft a story. If you have a set of dice for Table Top RPGs, roll two ten sided dice, using the first die for the tens digit, and the second die for the ones digit. For example: if you roll a 2 and a 7, the result is 27. Do this for each list.

Objects

1. Prosthetic eyeball
2. Boomerang made of bone
3. Set of rear-view mirror red fuzzy dice
4. Overcooked t-bone steak
5. Car battery
6. Pocketknife
7. Moonrock
8. Cursed porcelain doll head
9. Laptop filled with computer viruses
10. Book that tells you one thing that will happen tomorrow and updates while you sleep each night
11. Stick of bacon flavored bubble gum
12. Quilt made from heavy metal t-shirts
13. Three candles of different lengths and colors
14. Folding card table with one bent leg
15. Crate of audio cassette tapes with only dates written on their edges

16. Gallon of large curd cottage cheese
17. Meat cleaver with a yellow happy face sticker on the blade
18. Tomato
19. Invisible apple corer
20. Shoehorn made from an executed serial killer's tibia
21. Wrist watch with no hour hand
22. Latex glove filled with blueberry juice
23. Dull scissors
24. An inherited car that does not run
25. Extra left shoes
26. Expired coupon to the sex shop
27. Flail
28. Rusty key
29. Sentient dishwasher
30. Flashlight that reveals secrets
31. Fossilized fecal matter, coprolite
32. Your neighbor's artificial Christmas tree
33. Plate of scrambled eggs
34. Bowl of potato salad

35. Birth certificate for your eggplant

36. Farmer's almanac for next year

37. Pre-chewed bubble gum

38. Handheld barcode scanner

39. Pogo stick

40. Desert camouflage bandana

41. Cube die that only has 5 sides
    when counted

42. Stolen artifact

43. Gravedigger's shovel

44. Bottle of formaldehyde

45. Single cotton ball

46. Vacuum canister full of dog hair

47. Bag of psilocybin

48. Bag of portobello mushrooms

49. Bag of prosthetic ears

50. Gold crown from a molar

51. Ice axe

52. Hammer that no longer will
    function as a hammer

53. Nail file

54. Permanent marker

55. Invisible ink

56. Trans-dimensional key

57. Tooth from a medieval saint

58. Jar of chocolate pudding

59. Peppermint candy

60. Laser pointer

61. Laser gun

62. Fully automatic egg launcher

63. Severed human tongue

64. Potato

65. Smelly basketball

66. Talking hamster

67. Wobbly barstool

68. Five gallon bucket of maple syrup

69. Geiger counter

70. Cursed screwdriver

71. Pancake griddle

72. Ancient fruitcake

73. Thermos filled with ostrich blood

74. Spray paint

75. Box of rusty thumb tacks

76. Anxiety in physical form

77. Pat of butter

78. Your umbilical cord

79. Concrete evidence of life on Venus

80. Existential dread

81. Acoustic guitar with only two
     strings
82. John Bonham's drum key
83. Pet sphinx
84. Bike made in a country that does
     not exist
85. Blank sheet of paper
86. Fresh coat of paint
87. Twenty pounds of aluminum cans
88. Porcelain doll filled with dimes
89. Locket inherited from a
     grandmother
90. Portable wormhole
91. Too many puppies
92. Hot rod
93. Earthworm
94. Bongos
95. Lectern
96. Conductor's baton
97. Antique bugle
98. Megalodon tooth
99. Strip of yellow wallpaper
100. Backyard shed with chains bolted
     to the wall

Characters

1. Chef with a shellfish allergy
2. Mosquito
3. Dog who thinks he's a cat
4. Pig fresh bought from the county fair
5. Loaf of bread
6. Painter who is afraid of the color red
7. Grocery bagger
8. Man going through a mid-life crisis
9. Lumberjack whose limbs fall off on occasion
10. Middle-aged man with a fear of pastries
11. That one dude
12. Film critic
13. Social media influencer
14. Quality control at a fish cannery
15. CEO of startup company
16. Health inspector
17. Orc
18. Bank security guard

19. Student at middle school
20. Principal at middle school
21. Stay-at-home dad
22. Playground equipment tester
23. Your neighbor
24. Your celebrity crush
25. You
26. Dude who wrote this book
27. Esteemed actor Nicolas Cage
28. Bookseller at a small town book shop
29. Bookseller at a chain bookstore
30. Prison librarian
31. Drug testing lab technician
32. Pediatrist
33. Recently laid off tech worker
34. College student addicted to...
35. Gravedigger
36. Crooked pawn shop proprietor
37. Crooked pet shop proprietor
38. Receptionist at Assassins For Hire business
39. Squeamish owner of a funeral home

40. Person afraid of own shadow
41. Toothpick eater
42. Drummer having trouble finding
    a band
43. Event organizer specializing in the
    occult
44. Bespoke washer board
    craftsperson
45. Accountant with and extra finger on
    their dominant hand
46. Pottery instructor
47. Person with a record setting
    collection of...
48. Really bad magician
49. Demon pretending to be a Reno
    magician
50. That one dude staring at you
    right now
51. Pilot
52. Highly paid dominatrix
53. Super hero with a mundane super
    power
54. Steamboat Willie
55. Socrates

56. Evil doppelgänger

57. Ineffective anti-hero

58. Dolphin from Mars

59. Billy, the ultimate warrior

60. Lunchlady

61. Drum major

62. Sentient sex toy

63. Obsessive spray-tan addict

64. Punk rock musician

65. Retired television commercial actor

66. Small engine repair person

67. Spaceship plumbing specialist

68. Disgruntled zoo keeper

69. Movie projectionist

70. Duke of Albuquerque

71. Cheddar Master

72. Inventor of a new kind of fabric

73. Steam powered robot

74. Human who thinks they are a dog

75. Dog who thinks they are human

76. Body builder who does religious
    inspirational presentations

77. Con artist

78. Burlesque dancer

79. Roller derby champion

80. Mayor

81. Tarot reader

82. Road construction flagger

83. Chain smoker

84. Used car dealer

85. Physical therapist

86. Disgraced CEO

87. Tree surgeon

88. Inter dimensional traveller

89. Demon

90. Angel

91. Video game speed runner

92. Architectural consultant

93. Copyeditor

94. Dude with a wood chipper

95. Assistant cinematographer

96. Rare text restoration expert

97. Recent apostate

98. Fluffy, destroyer of worlds

99. Animated porcelain doll

100. One of the authors of this book

1. Local, most hip grocery store in town
2. Backyard of the local high school principle
3. Lab specializing in sperm count tests
4. Sex shop inspired by a store that rhymes with Shmarper Schwimage
5. Sex shop known for its large selection of non-anatomical and extreme sex toys
6. Vegan sausage factory
7. Break room at a 'big-box' store
8. Fish hatchery
9. Bar that only serves Country Themed cocktails
10. Community bike repair shop
11. Donut shop with horrible customer service
12. Call center for a life insurance money that is pretty much 100% known to be laundering money

13. Seventeen miles into an Alpine-like backpacking trip in the North Cascade Mountains of Washington state

14. Catering kitchen at a convention for professional butchers

15. Wherever you are right now

16. Your absolute favorite restaurant

17. Subway station where the public bathrooms have a sewage backup problem

18. Unfinished housing development abandoned after the housing market crash of 2008

19. Watch/clock repair shop

20. Big city mall in the late 1980s

21. Big city mall last year

22. Food truck fair

23. Inside a refrigerator box

24. Indie documentary film festival

25. Trade show for deli meat slicers

26. Pittsburgh

27. Your bathroom

28. Tomorrow at your day job

29. Lost in a forest

30. Kitchen of a major fast food chain

31. Schmamazon warehouse

32. Dilapidated cabin hidden in the woods

33. Castle ruins in Kansas

34. Beer garden

35. Drive-in movie theater

36. Main Street in small town Oklahoma

37. Museum of art

38. Museum of forgotten history

39. Walk-in spine replacement clinic

40. Inside the head of an erotica writer who is sitting in a coffee shop

41. Waiting room at the dentist

42. Candy factory on the verge of bankruptcy

43. The country fair after everything is closed for the night

44. In line for the cross continental train

45. Church service on Mars

46. Cafe run inside a brothel

47. Gym in Hell

48. International Space Station

49. Riding a ski lift

50. Public transit bus

51. Wig store

52. Abandoned funeral home

53. Classic malt shop

54. 1980s themed diner

55. Writer's room for a TV show about
    to be cut from production

56. Combination arcade and baked
    potato bar

57. Combination post office and hair
    salon

58. Combination pot shop and
    pie shop

59. 1990s video rental store

60. Cemetery

61. Mausoleum

62. Gothic castle converted into a
    gaudy tourist attraction

63. Ski resort during the off season
    with no snow

64. Island the size of a football field

65. Dragon training grounds

66. Top secret culinary school

67. Personal home of your favorite writer

68. Sardine cannery

69. Rentable orgy venue

70. Isolated in a huge greenhouse for science ('Viva los bio-dome!')

71. Onboard a deep sea submarine

72. Disco club

73. Backstage of a prestigious theater

74. World's worst patisserie

75. Homecoming football game

76. School bus

77. Community college art class

78. Autopsy room

79. Inside a colossal snail shell

80. On a road trip

81. Truck stop

82. Huge city in a fantasy setting

83. Golf course

84. Cultist lair

85. Scandinavian furniture store

86. Your backyard

87. Purple (Yes, the color. Deal with it.)

88. Remote mountain range

89. On a glacier

90. US / Canada border crossing

91. In a psychedelic/progressive rock album cover art

92. Haunted house

93. Olympic National Park

94. Charon's boat on the River Styx

95. Potato farm

96. Organ farm

97. Portland, Oregon

98. Swamp

99. Theme park in Purgatory

100. On the battlefield in the midst of a huge kerfuffle between cyborgs and dinosaurs.

Acknowledgments

First of all, I would like to thank all of the contributors to this book of prompts. This would not exist if it were not for you. Also, lots and lots of thanks to all of those who make BizarroCon happen. Us writers of the "weird stuff" need a place to call our own, and BizarroCon is just that.

And, as always, thank you so much to my beautiful wife, Melissa. I would never be able to tackle any of my creative projects without you to cheer me on. Love you!

—Joe

About J.W. Donley

 **J.W. Donley**—HWA and HOWL Society member —lives with his family in the Pacific Northwest where the Cascade Mountains meet the Salish Sea. J.W. is the author of the novelette *Cats of the Pacific Northwest* and the brand new *100 Unusual Prompts for Writers of Horror, Weird, and Bizarro Fiction* with contributions from John Langan, Carlton Mellick III, Shane Hawk, and many more. His short stories have appeared in anthologies from Dim Shores, HOWL Society Press, PIT, Chuckanut Editions, and on Creepy, a Horror Podcast.

About the Contributors

John Baltisberger is an award-winning author of genre fiction that often focuses on violent and psychedelic elements. He also runs the Splatterpunk/Bizarro publishing house, Madness Heart Press.

Patrick Barb is an author of weird, dark, and horrifying tales, currently living (and trying not to freeze to death) in Saint Paul, Minnesota. His published works include the

dark fiction collection *Pre-Approved for Haunting* (Keylight Books), the novellas *Gargantuana's Ghost* (Grey Matter Press) and *Turn* (Alien Buddha Press), as well as the novelette *Helicopter Parenting in the Age of Drone Warfare* (Spooky House Press). His forthcoming works include the themed short-story collection *The Children's Horror* (Northern Republic Press) and the sci-fi/horror novel *Abducted* (Dark Matter Ink). Visit him at patrickbarb.com.

Bridget D. Brave writes weird and whimsical horror from the foothills of the St. Francois mountains. She can be found nearly everywhere online @beedeebrave.

Garrett Cook is a Wonderland Award winning author and editor of Horror and Bizarro fiction. His latest is *Charcoal* from CLASH

Books, now available at retailers and on Audible.

Shane Hawk (enrolled Cheyenne-Arapaho, Hidatsa and Citizen Potawatomi descent) is a history teacher by day and a horror writer by night. Hawk's literary contributions include his debut story collection, *Anoka*, alongside short fiction featured in numerous anthologies. He recently co-edited *Never Whistle at Night*, an internationally bestselling Indigenous dark fiction anthology published by Penguin Random House. Hawk lives in San Diego, California with his beautiful wife. Learn more at <u>shanehawk.com</u>.

S.A. Hunt is an award-winning novelist and Army veteran living in the darkest corners of northern Michigan. Her bestselling *Malus*

Domestica horror-action series has been translated into German and is published worldwide.

Frances Lu-Pai Ippolito is a writer, judge, and mother. When she's not spending time with her family outdoors in the Pacific Northwest, she's crafting short stories in horror, sci-fi, fantasy, or whatever genre-bending she can get away with. Her stories have appeared in Nailed Magazine, Buckman Journal's Issue 006, and will be included in upcoming anthologies. Her work was also featured in the *Ooligan Press Writers of Color Showcase 2020* in Portland, Oregon.

In her free time, she serves as a first reader for magazines, volunteers with her local writing group, Willamette Writers, and has a particular interest in mentoring youth and young writers. She's also a member of the Horror Writers Association, Society of

Children's Book Writers and Illustrators, and Northwest Independent Writer's Association.

Ai Jiang is a Chinese-Canadian writer, Ignyte Award winner, Hugo, Astounding, Nebula, Locus, Bram Stoker, and BSFA Award  finalist, and an immigrant from Fujian currently residing in Toronto, Ontario. Her work can be found in F&SF, The Dark, Uncanny, The Masters Review, among others. She is the recipient of Odyssey Workshop's 2022 Fresh Voices Scholarship and the author of *Linghun* and *I AM AI*. The first book of her novella duology, *A Palace Near the Wind,* is forthcoming 2025 with Titan Books. Find her on X (@AiJiang_), Insta (@ai.jian.g), and online (http://aijiang.ca).

 **C.B. Jones** is an author from somewhere in the middle of America. He is the author of the books *The Rules of*

the Road and *Crybaby Bridge: Slaughter in a Small Town.*

John Langan is the author of two novels and five collections of fiction. For his work, he has received the the Bram Stoker and This Is Horror awards. He lives in

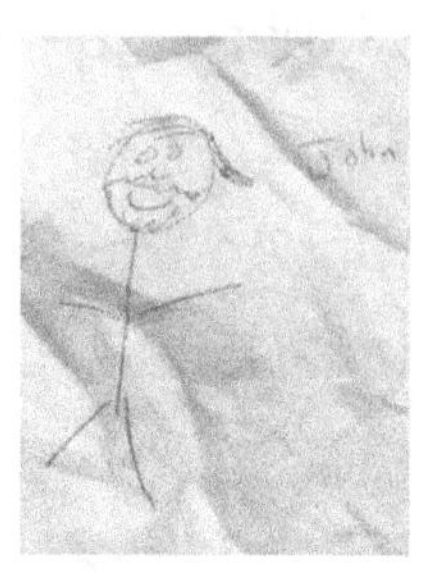

New York's Mid-Hudson valley with his wife, younger son, and a rather sizable goldfish.

P.L. McMillan's short fiction has appeared in a variety of anthologies and maga-zines such as *Cosmic Horror Monthly, Strange Lands Short Stories, Negative Space,* and *AHH! That's What I Call Horror,* as well as adapted to audio forms for podcasts like NoSleep and Nocturnal Trans-missions. In addition to her short stories, McMillan's debut collection, *What Remains When The Stars Burn Out,* and debut novella,

Sisters of the Crimson Vine, are available now.

Besides being a fiction writer, PLM has experience as an editor (*Howls from the Dark Ages* and *The Darkness Beyond The Stars: An Anthology of Space Horror*), hosts PLM Talks on Youtube (interviewing peers and professionals in the horror industry), and is the co-host of a horror writing craft podcast, Dead Languages Podcast. On top of all that, PLM does digital illustrations and artwork for anthologies and her merch shop.

Brianna Malotke is a writer based in the Pacific Northwest. In addition to being a member and on the social media team for the Horror Writers Association, she's also co-chair of the Seattle Chapter. She has work in *Beautiful Tragedies 2 and 3, The Dire Circle, The Nottingham Horror Collective, Under Her Skin,* and *HorrorScope: A Zodiac Anthology*

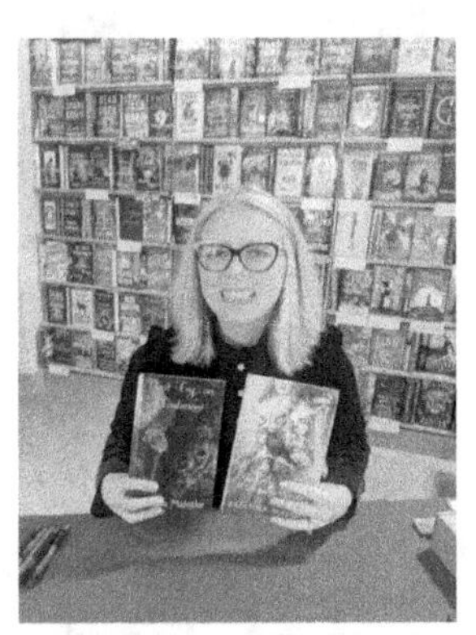

Volumes 1 and 4. In fall of 2023 her debut horror poetry collection, *Fashion Trends, Deadly Ends*, was released and she was a "Writer in Residence" at the Chateau d'Orquevaux in France. Malotke's next collection, *Lost Cherry*, will be published with January Ember Press fall of 2024.

Carlton Mellick III has made a living writing bizarro fiction novels to a cult audience for over twenty years. His work has been translated into German, Spanish, Italian, Czech, Polish, Russian, Turkish, Persian, French and Japanese. He lives on the Washington Coast.

Christi Nogle is the author of the Shirley Jackson Award nominated and Bram Stoker Award® winning first novel *Beulah* (Cemetery

Gates Media) and three short fiction collections, the Stoker-nominated *The Best of Our Past, the Worst of Our Future*; *Promise: A Collection of Weird Science Fiction*; and *One Eye Opened in That Other Place* (Flame Tree Press). Her work has also appeared in over fifty publications including *PseudoPod*, *Three-Lobed Burning Eye*, and *Vastarien*. Follow her at https://christinogle.com/ and on across social media as christinogle.

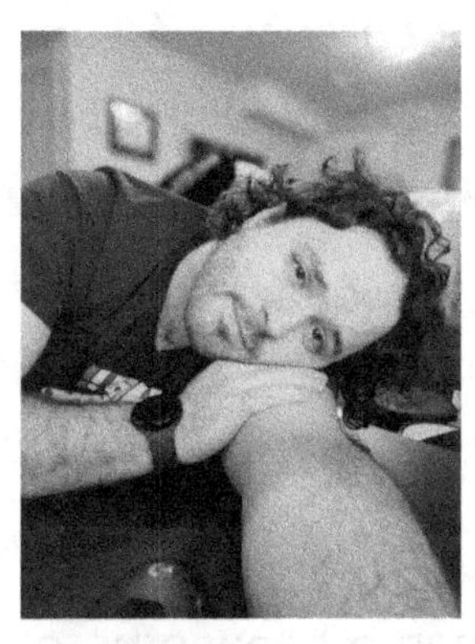

Christopher O'Halloran (he/him) is the factory-working, Canadian, actor-turned-author of *Pushing Daisy*, his upcoming debut novel from Lethe Press (2025). His shorter work has been published or forthcoming from Kaleidotrope, NoSleep Podcast, Cosmic Horror Monthly, and others. He is editor of the anthology, *Howls from the Wreckage*. Visit

COauthor.ca for stories, reviews, and updates on upcoming novels.

TJ Price's corporeal being is currently located in Raleigh, NC, where he lives with his handsome partner of many years, but his ghosts can be found in northeastern Connecti-

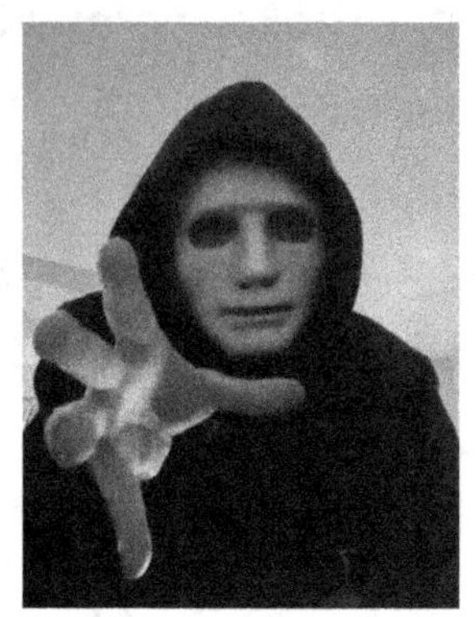

cut, southern Maine, and north Brooklyn. He is the author of *The Disappearance of Tom Nero*, a novelette, and has work published in venues such as Nightmare Magazine, pidgeonholes, The NoSleep Podcast, as well as various anthologies and assorted grimoires. He can be invoked at either tjpricewrites.com, or go to the darkest place you know and whisper his name. Please note: the author is not responsible for what may answer.

Chelsea Pumpkins is a Massachusetts writer of strange, chilling, and sometimes sad fiction and a fan of all things macabre. She is

a hiker, an animal lover, and considers herself a foodie but has absolutely no standards when it comes to mac and cheese. You can read her stories in various horror anthologies, Shortwave Magazine, and Cosmic Horror Monthly. She is the editor of *AHH! That's What I Call Horror: An Anthology of '90s Horror*, and a co-host of The Cutthroat Queens podcast. Learn more about her work at chelseapumpkins.com and follow her on social media @chelseapumpkins.

Sam Rebelein holds an MFA in Creative Writing from Goddard College, with a focus on Horror and Memoir. His work has appeared in *Bourbon*

Penn, PseudoPod, Gamut, Press Pause

Press, Ellen Datlow's *Best Horror of the Year,* and elsewhere. Sam's debut horror novel *Edenville* is out now from William Morrow. His follow-up collection of stories set in the same fictional universe, *The Poorly Made and Other Things,* is coming for you in early 2025. For more about Sam's work (and pictures of his dog), find him on Instagram @rebelsam94.

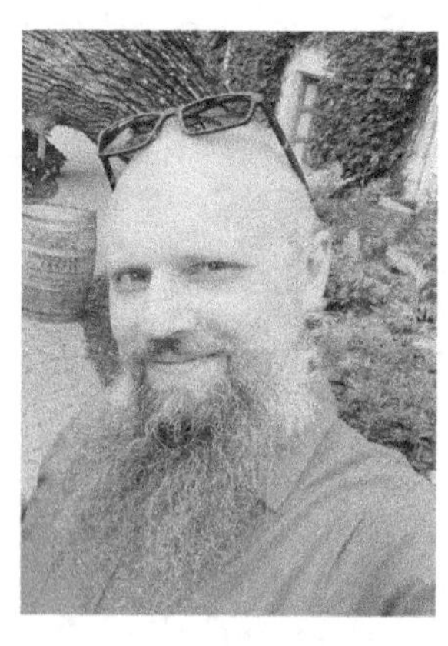

Michael Allen Rose is an award-winning writer, musician, editor and performance artist based in Chicago, Illinois. His stories have appeared in The Magazine of Bizarro Fiction, Heavy Feather Review, and Tales From The Crust among other periodicals. He has published several books including *Jurassichrist* (Perpetual Motion Machine Publishing) which won the 2021 Wonderland Award for best bizarro novel, and *The Last 5 Minutes of the Human Race,*

winner of best collection in bizarro fiction 2022. He is the host of the annual Ultimate Bizarro Showdown at Bizarro Con in Oregon. Michael also releases industrial music under the name Flood Damage. He lives with an awesome cat named Dr. Light, and enjoys good tea. You can find more at <u>www.michaelallenrose.com</u>

Schism is an illustrator working in Cape Town. Her work can be found at www.instagram.com/schism.art.

Caleb Stephens is an award-winning author writing

from

somewhere deep in the Colorado mountains. His short stories have appeared in multiple publications and podcasts. He is also the author of *Feeders,* a speculative horror thriller available through Timber Ghost Press, and *The Girls in the Cabin*, a psychological thriller available through Joffe Books. His dark fiction collection *If Only a Heart and Other Tales of Terror* is available through Salt Heart Press and includes the short story "The Wallpaper Man," which was adapted to film by Falconer Film & Media in 2022. You can join his mailing list and learn more at www.calebstephensauthor.com as well as follow him on Instagram @caleb-stephensauthor.

Angela Sylvaine is a self-proclaimed cheerful goth who writes speculative fiction and poetry. Her debut novel, *Frost Bite*, a '90s sci-fi horror comedy, and her debut short

story collection, *The Dead Spot: Stories of Lost Girls* are available now. Her short fiction and poetry have appeared in or on over fifty anthologies, magazines, and podcasts, including *Southwest Review*, *Apex,* and *The NoSleep Podcast.* She lives in the shadow of the Rocky Mountains with her sweetheart and three creepy cats. You can find her online <u>angelasylvaine.com</u>.

Richard Thomas is the award-winning author of nine books: four novels—*Incarnate* (Podium), *Breaker* and *Disintegration* (Penguin Random House Alibi), and *Transubstantiate*; four short story collections—*Spontaneous Human Combustion* (Turner Publishing—Bram Stoker finalist), *Tribulations* (Cemetery Dance), *Staring Into the Abyss*, and *Herniated Roots*; as well as one novella of *The Soul Standard* (Dzanc Books). His over 175 stories in print include *The Best Horror of the Year* (Volume Eleven), *Cemetery Dance* (twice), *Behold!: Oddities, Curiosities and Undefinable Wonders* (Bram Stoker Award winner), *The Hideous Book of Hidden Horrors* (Shirley Jackson Award winner), *Lightspeed, PANK, storySouth, Gargoyle, Weird Fiction Review, Midwestern Gothic, Shallow Creek, The Seven Deadliest,*

Gutted: Beautiful Horror Stories, Qualia Nous (#1&2)„ *Chiral Mad* (#2-4), *PRISMS, Pantheon,* and *Shivers VI.* He was also the editor of four anthologies: *The New Black* and *Exigencies* (Dark House Press), *The Lineup: 20 Provocative Women Writers* (Black Lawrence Press) and *Burnt Tongues* (Medallion Press) with Chuck Palahniuk. He has been nominated for the Bram Stoker (twice), Shirley Jackson, Thriller, and Audie awards. In his spare time he is a columnist at Lit Reactor. He is currently the Editor-in-Chief at *Gamut* and also ran Dark House Press. For more information visit <u>www.whatdoes-notkillme.com</u> or contact Paula Munier at Talcott Notch.

Clay Vermulm, born on the frigid, windswept plains of Cut Bank, Montana, has set down proverbial roots in the  Pacific Northwest where he likes to climb rocks on the days it's not raining. For the other ninety-eight percent of the year, he enjoys writing, reading, and playing board games with his partner Deanna as his cat criticizes his every life decision from her carpeted tree palace.

Clay is the author of *Crevasse*, *Blue Rare and Other Short Stories*, and the editor of the recent collection *Bad Spirits* with Tori V. Rainn. He is the program coordinator for the Seattle HWA, the Secretary for Cascade Writers, and a member of several other writing organizations.

Carson Winter is an award-winning author, punker, and raw nerve. His fiction has been featured in *Apex, Vastarien,* and *Tales to Terrify*. His novel *The Psychographist* is out now from Apocalypse Party Press. He co-hosts the horror writing craft podcast Dead Languages. You can find Carson under gray skies and a curtain of rain in the Pacific Northwest.

Images Credits

- 'Brain' image
  by <u>Colleen</u> from <u>Pixabay'</u>
- 'Banana' image by Kimona from Pexels
- Computer Parade to mark the 750th anniversary of Berlin. Berlin, 1987 | Thomas Uhlemann, Bundesarchiv | CC BY-SA
- Head on a plate Photo by Designecologist: Pexels
- Skull, Image by <u>OpenClipart-Vectors</u> from <u>Pixabay</u>

- Femur, Image
  by b0red from Pixabay